A LOCAL HISTORY OF POONA AND ITS BATTLEFIELDS

A LOCAL HISTORY OF POONA AND ITS BATTLEFIELDS

COLONEL L. W. SHAKESPEAR

WITH ILLUSTRATIONS

GYAN

Published by

Gyan Publishing House
5, Ansari Road
Daryaganj, New Delhi-110002
Phone: 011-47034999, 9811692060
E-mail: books@gyanbooks.com

Distribution Network
gyanbooks.com
India, USA, Canada, UK, Australia, France

ISBN : 978-81-212-9657-1 (PB)
First Published, 1916

2nd Impression 2023

Printed at: Gyan Press, Delhi.

A LOCAL HISTORY OF POONA AND ITS BATTLEFIELDS
Author: COLONEL L. W. SHAKESPEAR

A LOCAL HISTORY OF POONA

AND ITS BATTLEFIELDS

BY

COLONEL L. W. SHAKESPEAR

(A.Q.M.G. 6TH POONA DIVISION)

AUTHOR OF

"HISTORY OF THE 2ND K.E.O. GOORKHAS"

AND "HISTORY OF UPPER ASSAM AND THE NORTH-EAST FRONTIER"

WITH ILLUSTRATIONS

1916

THIS BRIEF HISTORICAL SKETCH OF POONA AND ITS NEIGHBOURHOOD IS RESPECTFULLY DEDICATED TO THEIR EXCELLENCIES LORD AND LADY WILLINGDON, WHOSE INTEREST IN THE SUBJECT HAS ENCOURAGED THE AUTHOR IN HIS HUMBLE EFFORTS TO AROUSE A LIKE FEELING AMONG OTHER SOJOURNERS IN THIS PART OF THE DECCAN

PREFACE

KNOWING there must be many others far more knowledgeable than myself in these matters of local history, I venture on this subject with diffidence in the hope that, though an abler pen might have made more of it, and in spite of its possible faults, it may prove of interest to those whose lives are cast in this historic locality.

L. W. SHAKESPEAR.

POONA,
September 1915.

ILLUSTRATIONS

	PAGE
View of the Old Residency, City, and Parbatti Hill in 1809	*Frontispiece*
One of the old Houses of the "Gārpir" Cantonment	15
Earliest English Cemetery near St. Paul's Church	16
Last of the Masonry Sentry-boxes of the old Gārpir Cantonment	17
Front View of the curious "Pānchleshwari" Temple (Hindu) at Bambūrda, Poona	21
Side View of "Pānchleshwari" Temple, looking down on the Mandap and showing the rock-cut cistern	23
Scindia's Wāri near Wanowri	42
Entrance to Scindia's Wāri	43
Corner in Poona City	45
Entrance to Shānāwāri Palace in Poona City	47
Walls and Bastions of the Shānāwāri Palace	48
Entrance to Vishrambagh Palace in Poona City	49
Temple on Parbatti Hill	50
View of Parbatti Hill from the Hira Bagh	52
Tombs of French Officers on the Shankerseth Road	53
Ruins of the Peishwa's Palace on Parbatti Hill	54
The Memorial at Korigaon	56
Ruins of Main Gate, Chākun Fort	58
Phirūngaji's Bastion, Chākun Fort	60
Colonel Deacon's Breach, Chākun Fort	63

PAGE

Ancient Stone Burial Circle at Bhosari . . . 64
View of the Konkan Darwaza at Singarh, breached by the English in March 1818 67
Memorial Stone to Tannaji Malūsre in Singarh Fort . 69
The Poona Gate at Singarh Fort 70
View along the Great Dam of the Karakwasla Lake, below Singarh 71
East Wall of Sāswad Palace with English cannon-shot holes of March 1818 73
General View of Purandhar Hill and Fortress . . 74
View of Wazigarah Hill looking down on Convalescent Depot from south-east bastion of Purandhar . 75
Temples at Sāswad 76
Temple in Sāswad Palace 77
Interior of Chaitya at Karli 84
Entrance in hill-side to the Karli Chaitya . . 85
Dāgobas cut out of the rocky hill-side at Bhāja . 87
Interior of Induri Fort and Main Gate . . . 89
Induri Fort from the river 91
The Upper Gateway at Lohgarh Fort 94
The Spur at Lohgarh Fort with Sheikh Avālia's Spear-hole 95
Aurangzeb's ruined Cenotaph at Lohgarh . . . 96
View looking down on the "Scorpion's Tail" Rock . 97

PLANS

(From Blacker's *Mahratta Wars.*)

FACE PAGE

Battle of Kirkee 30
Combat at Yerrowda Ford 34
Action at Korigaon 56
Attack on Chākun Fort 62
Attack on Singarh Fort 68

BIBLIOGRAPHY

J. Douglas's Work on Bombay.

Grant Duff's "History of the Mahrattas."

J. Douglas's "Stray Papers on Western India."

Ed. Lake's "Sieges of the Madras Army."

"Life of Wellington."

Gazetteer of Poona.

Broughton's "Letters from a Mahratta Camp," 1809.

Blacker's "History of the Mahratta Campaigns," 1821.

Orme's "History of India."

Col. Newnham Smith's Notes on the Poona Cantonment.

Biddulph's "Pirates of the Malabar Coast."

Notes on Transactions in the Mahratta Empire, 1803.

Lord Valentia's Travels in the East from 1802 to 1806.

Bishop Heber's Diary of Travel in India, 1824–25.

Ferguson's Indian Archaeology.

POONA

BRIEF EARLY HISTORY

THE interest of this district of which Poona is now the chief city is great, both for those fond of ancient history and for those more disposed to learn of our own doings in these parts. It is not intended to go deep into dynastic matters, but only to touch on the locality's earliest days, and then turn to more modern times; calling up items of interest which may make their sojourn here, and perhaps their outings, of greater value to present-day residents.

In the far-off past this district was largely concerned with religion, as evidenced by the vast number of Buddhist and Hindu temples and monastic cells carved into the solid rock, attesting wonderful trouble and patience of those old-time peoples, also, it may be supposed, unlimited labour; from which we may infer it was well populated. We find evidences of old trade routes leading from the seaports of those days, Kalyan and Sopara, into the centre of India as existing in the second century B.C. Such evidences are inscriptions cut into the rock at some of these temples, and others which may be seen at the two most notable early Passes, viz. Mālsej and Nāna, leading down from the plateau through the Ghats to the Konkan below, and which lie a little west of Jūnnar, fifty odd miles north of Poona, the oldest city in this part of the Deccan. That the Bhor Ghat was also largely used in those days by traders is shown by groups of cave-temples in its vicinity, also what were rest-chambers and water-cisterns for the comfort of the travellers, cut out of the solid rock.

Although Poona is not actually mentioned in those early days, trade must have passed through its neighbourhood from these Passes; and as several routes met about here going from the Bombay side towards Hyderabad, and from the old Hindu Chalukyan capital of Vijyanagar (near Bellary) north towards Malwa, we can assume it was due to this that a small village gradually sprang into importance. The earliest accounts which show a settled organized community in these parts are those dealing with the ancient Andhra kingdom (Dravidian), which, starting a little north of Nellore on the Madras coast, consolidated itself and spread west over the whole area comprised between the Godāveri and Kistna rivers. In Asoka's edicts of 256 B.C. this kingdom is alluded to as being subject to his imperial commands, but enjoying a considerable amount of autonomy under its own kings. It is said it owned 30 walled towns (names not given), and had an army of 100,000 foot, 30,000 cavalry, and 1000 elephants. If that was so, it is not to be wondered that, on Asoka's death, the Andhra dynasty extended its sway beyond Nasik even to Sopara, the seaport of greatest importance then on this part of the west coast, and lying some twenty miles north of Bombay. This dynasty came to an end during the early part of the second century A.D., after an existence of four and a half centuries as a power, according to the testimony of the lists in the *Matsya Purānas* or dynastic lists of the fifth century B.C.

To the Andhras are ascribed the marvellous rock-cut religious works so plentifully found in the hills from Nasik to Poona, as well as those on Elephanta Island, Bombay, and the inscriptions found at Sopara—all testifying to the depth of Buddhist and Brahminical Hinduism in their earlier and purer stages. That they were a literate people is shown by their knowledge of Prākrit, an earlier form of the Pāli writing, in which they carved their inscriptions into the living rock, sometimes recording events, sometimes matter for public instruction—in which latter case we find these placed in suitable positions on highways or at frequented places of pilgrimage. Silver coins of the later Andhra kings have been found at Sopara and Jūnnar, and the first foreigner to record his visit to these parts is the Chinese traveller, Fāhien, about A.D. 405, who speaks of the people as being "capable, industrious, and sincere observers of the Laws of Piety."

It is surmised that some of the larger hill-fortresses were built in those far-off days, particularly Purandhar and Singarh near Poona and Shivner near Jūnnar, which latter saw the birth of Sivaji, the real founder of Maharatta power and state.

From about A.D. 230 to A.D. 500 no specific information is found concerning this locality; but there is reason to believe that the western or Poona portion was ruled by the Ratta or Reddi clan, which in the middle of the eighth century became sufficiently powerful as to be styled "Maharasthra," or country of the greater Rattas, from whence the present name Maharatta. One tradition says these Reddis came originally from the Canara country, and were the best fighting folk in the Carnatic; another gives them a northern origin.

The end of the thirteenth century saw the Mohamedans moving south from Delhi to crush the Yādav power which had latterly arisen. These people built the stupendous hill-fortress of Deoghir (now Daulatabad) near Aurangabad. Ferishta, in his Moghul history, records how "numbers of the men of Abu Suba's (Gujerati) force, when halted in the neighbourhood, went off to visit a remarkable and famous fortified mountain called Deoghir, which city was near at hand." This is about the earliest notice we have of Deoghir, and from Buddhist remains on the citadel hill its importance was evidently of great antiquity as a place of religion and residence. The Deccan was invaded, but it took thirty-five years of war to crush the Yādavs, and the first record of stirring interest in the vicinity of our Poona is noted by the same historian Ferishta in 1340, when Mahomed Tuglak of Delhi, having settled his new capital at Daulatabad, sent a large force against Khōndāna (the present Singarh),

15 miles south of Poona. This shows that Singarh must have been a place of considerable importance in those days to warrant such action against it. It is recorded this fortress was defended with great bravery, and Mahomed after several fruitless assaults had to blockade the place, which after eight months brought about the capitulation of the Ratta Chief.

The end of the next century we hear of the forts of Singarh and Lohgarh near Lonauli being again besieged and taken by the Mahomedans, as the revolting Maharattas had seized and garrisoned them; but it is not till 1604 that, according to Grant Duff, we hear of Poona actually, and then only as a pergunna which with that of Chākun, 21 miles out on the Nasik road, was made over by the Ahmednagar court to Malloji Bhonsla, the grandfather of Sivaji. About 1637 Malloji's son Shahji first made his residence in Poona village, becoming a wealthy man on being rewarded by the Mahomedans for services in the Carnatic, by an extension of his jaghir to include the hill country south of Poona and known as the "Māwuls." By the time his son the famous Sivaji was able to begin his offensive actions against the hated Mahomedan, Poona had increased, and contained buildings of sufficient strength for defence, although it was never a walled and fortified town. Another Moghul historian, Khāfi Khan, speaks of it in Aurungzeb's day as "situated on a treeless plain"—very different from its present well-wooded state. Sivaji's life was, however, chiefly spent at Satāra, or else on expeditions or amongst his favourite hill-forts Torna and Raigarh, west of Singarh, both of which he built.

It may be stated here that the first time English troops came into touch at all with the Maharattas was in a friendly way in the middle of the eighteenth century, when both Governments combined in efforts to rid themselves of the presence of Toolaji Angria, the notorious sea pirate, whose depredations along the coast, and even sometimes inland, had become intolerable, and trade suffered. The Maharattas hunted Angria's people on land, while we, for the time being, overcame them on the sea. Their final overthrow was at Geriah on the Konkan coast, a stronghold besieged by Admiral Watson and Colonel Clive with a fleet, together with a Maharatta force on land. After a stubborn defence the place fell, and ended the days of the pirates of the west coast.[1] It was

[1] The booty which fell to the English was most extensive, including £130,000 worth of gold, silver, and jewels; and it was here

this success in 1755 which really raised the English to political importance in this part of India.

Sivaji, the founder of Maharatta power and contemporary of Mr. Aungier our first Governor of Bombay in 1669, is usually spoken of as a swashbuckler and murderer; but, however true this may be to a certain extent, he had characteristics which lift him out of that category. Besides being a first-rate rider, swordsman, and marksman, he was noted for great filial affection and for remarkable consideration and respect towards women. Unlike his decadent successors, however, he would never allow a woman in or near his camps when he and his army took the field; and it used then to be said of him that he would rather hear the neighing of his enemies' horses than a woman's voice. Historians tell of the great fascination he possessed over women, and certainly the rather pathetic story of Zaib ul Nissa, daughter of the Emperor Aurangzeb and Sivaji's inveterate enemy, seems to uphold the fact. Nissa saw him when a prisoner in

that Clive, although a poor man then, to show his disinterestedness in money, and to help a brother officer in need, gave up his share of the prize-money (£1000),—thus early, as it were, justifying his boast years after as to his amazing moderation when practically the treasures of Bengal were at his command.

Delhi and fell in love with him. Later during a short period of comparative peace, Aurangzeb did offer his daughter in marriage with a view to cementing friendship, but Sivaji declined, as he would not turn from his own religion to marry her. Nissa never married, and followed her father about the Deccan in hopes of a meeting with Sivaji which never came off. After the great Maharatta's death Aurangzeb's forces succeeded in storming the fortress of Raigarh, when amongst the prisoners captured was Sivaji's little grandson Shahoo. Nissa immediately took charge of the child and brought him up. She died at Brāhmāpūri on the Bhima river and was buried at Begumpur, 24 miles from Sholapore, where the Emperor raised a large mausoleum to her memory. Elphinstone says of Sivaji that " he left behind him a name and character such as has never been equalled or approached by any of his countrymen." So that, in spite of the general opinion as to his being a swashbuckler, bully, and murderer, there must have been a considerable amount of good in him.

Aurangzeb spent nearly twenty years in the Deccan trying hard to subdue the " mountain rat," as he called Sivaji, and failed. According to the Moghul historian Khāfi Khan, the Emperor said this of him, that "he was a great Captain, and the only one who has been able to raise a new kingdom while I have been trying to destroy the ancient sovereignties in India. My forces have been employed against him for nineteen years, nevertheless his State has increased."

Sivaji was singularly tolerant of religions other than his own, mosques and the Korān were never violated, and no one ever suffered death at his hands owing to their difference in religion. Compare this with what was going on in Europe at that period! All the same he was a past master in the art of duplicity, and his ruling passion was a love of amassing money. His famous sword "Bhowani," a fine Genoese blade inherited by one of his descendants the Raja of Kholapore, was presented by this noble to the Prince of Wales on his visit to India in 1874.

Sivaji's coronation and marriage took place at his favourite hill-fortress of Raigarh in the Konkan District, west of the Syhadri range and about three marches from Poona, in June 1674, and it was attended by a British Embassy from Bombay under Henry Oxenden, brother of Sir George Oxenden, Governor of Surat. This seems to be the first friendly visit on a large scale to the Maharatta Court, and Oxenden has left a vivid description of his journey there—the fatiguing climb, the heat just before the rains broke, the glorious views, the massive buildings and defences, and the magnificent ceremonies. Raigarh seems much connected with the life of the great Maharatta Chief: he built it and had to fight hard several times for its retention; it was from here he set out with 70,000 of his best troops on his memorable expedition to the Carnatic, where he levied tribute up to Madras; while his mother died here and so did he; being buried, Douglas tells us, amidst a holocaust of wives, elephants, and camels. His mausoleum stood there for numberless years neglected, covered with weeds and jungle growths, even the sacred Nandi in front of it having been allowed to topple over, until about 1885 when it was restored by Lord Reay. Raigarh was almost the last fort to fall to British troops after the overthrow of Bhaji Rao, last of the Peishwas and a descendant of Sivaji; and when Colonel Prothero's troops entered after bombarding the place in June 1818 and setting its buildings on fire, a native lady was found crouching in terror and despair alone amongst the embers of the conflagration. This was the favourite wife of Bhaji Rao, sent there for safety during the war. Her husband had already been sent a prisoner to Northern India, so it may be said that with her at Raigarh Maharatta power and influence vanished for ever; and rather calls to mind the engraving on a coin of the Emperor Vespasian—a woman sitting low in the dust under a palm-tree, and closing one of the last chapters of ancient history.

From Sivaji's day to that of the Peishwa, Ballāji Bhaji Rao, in whose time, about 1750, Poona, now greatly increased in size and importance, was acknowledged as the Maharatta capital, and who, it is said, planted a million mango trees in and about the town to beautify it, there is not much to concern us. The times were full of trouble and fighting for the Maharattas and Moghuls, which we pass over until 1755, when the success of the English and Maharatta combination against the celebrated sea pirate Angria, already mentioned, led to a visit to Poona of two members of the Bombay Council, Messrs. Spencer and Byfield. These interviewed the Peishwa on the subject of his desire to obtain the services of a body of English troops, which came to nothing until a few years later, when the English Government agreed to a brigade being located at Poona to assist the last Peishwa Bhaji Rao and keep him in power. In 1772 a Mr. Mostyn was definitely appointed Resident at the Court of Poona, and English troops numbering 3000 men were located there and took part in various actions as far south as Dharwar, under Colonels Frederick, Little, and others. These were later returned to Bombay owing to unsatisfactory dealings on the part of the Peishwa; but the Brigade was again sent to Poona later, when it was camped west of the Sangum, where the old Residency stood, until lines and houses were arranged for them on the ground in the vicinity of the present St. Paul's Church.

This brings us to a period when Poona began to possess a personal interest for the English, and in order the better to describe its history from now on, to touch on the many events of a stirring nature, and to make our outings more interesting, it would seem easiest to do so as if in a series of rides. So let us start our first outing from the great social centre, the Gymkhana Club, and proceed towards Ganeshkhind. Few, perhaps, know that in passing the Poona Hotel they enter the area covered from about 1780 to 1817 by the first Cantonment occupied by us with our Subsidiary Force, paid for by the Peishwa for his protection, and a set-off to French intrigues and growing influence. For those who do not know, I may explain that the Peishwa was the Prime Minister of the Maharatta Court in this part of the Deccan; the Raja residing at Satāra sank about 1714 into a religious or spiritual head, while the Peishwa wielded all temporal power. Bāllaji Vishwanath was the first to usurp this power, which was kept by his successors until the English obtained the upper hand. The same procedure of dual rule is still to be seen in Nepal, where the Maharaja Adiraj lives in religious seclusion, all affairs of state and war being attended to by the Prime Minister who is also Commander-in-Chief.

This old Cantonment extended roughly from the present Collector's Office to the Poona Hotel, and for some little distance south of the Jewish Synagogue, and at that time between these lines and the city, was a considerable stretch of open country, fields, and gardens. As we pass along the road from St. Paul's Church to the Sassoon Hospital a few of the old houses occupied by English officials in those long-past days can still be seen, built internally on a different scale from what we are accustomed to nowadays. The first English Cemetery is to be seen in a walled enclosure on the right of the road just before reaching the Bombay Bank, opposite which stood until July 1915 an old crumbling masonry

One of the old Houses of the "Gārpir" Cantonment, now used as a home and playground for students of the Byramji School of Medicine.

sentry-box, such as were in those days dotted along the outskirts of military lines. This Cantonment was known as "Gārpir," from the shrine to an old Mohamedan saint which is on the ground owned by the Bombay Bank, standing under trees to the left of the road, and almost opposite the old Cemetery.

It was in these lines that our troops stood to arms during the finale of the battle of Harapsa between Jeswant Rao Holkar, and Scindia and Bhaji Rao's combined forces—Scindia's beaten troops being pursued round the Cantonment, which was, however, not

Earliest English Cemetery near St. Paul's Church.

molested, the British flag being respected by both belligerents. The English were not concerned in this affair owing to a new treaty which had not been completed, and owing also to the Peishwa's recent disregard of the first treaty. It was from this Cantonment that Mr. Elphinstone in November 1817 withdrew our troops to camp on the open ground round

Kirkee village just before Bhaji Rao turned his army against us, as that ground was more favourable for defence than these lines, surrounded as they were by fields, gardens, and hedges. The moment these lines were vacated, the Maharattas pillaged and burnt the place,

Last of the Masonry Sentry-boxes of the old Gārpir Cantonment.

together with the Residency vacated by Mr. Elphinstone and Staff. The two curious old stone pillars, one in the Post Office compound and one in the open space near St. Paul's Church, are said to be the last of the stone posts to which the elephants were tied, and probably mark where the Transport Lines then were. Another idea is that they are the north and south stones to which the ropes of the Residency flag-staff were attached, the east and west ones having disappeared when the roadway was made past St. Paul's Church. Whichever they are really, it is known in early days that there was an elephant standing, and old Parsi residents declare the Duke of Wellington's animals were tethered on this spot.

Arriving in our ride at the Mūtha river and Sangam, and crossing the bridge, we are on the site of the first Residency built about early 1775 for Mr. Mostyn, the first British Envoy deputed to the Peishwa's Court by the Bombay Government. There is a rather good old-time coloured picture in the Western India Club by Henry Salt, showing the Sangam, or junction of the Mūtha and Mūla rivers, the City, and the Parbatti hill beyond, and the old-time Residency with the white flag and the red cross of St. George floating over it in the year 1809. It gives a good idea of what the river must have looked like before the big Bund was thrown across it lower down in the early "'thirties," and also of the extent of the city at that time.

J. Douglas tells us that in Sir Charles Malet's day, the Resident in Poona 1785–91, the

Residency was the pleasantest abode in India. Sir Charles built aqueducts, planted vines, apple- and peach-trees, kept a stud of Arab horses, and a number of elephants, in fact lived in a style suitable to the rank and dignity of the great nation he represented; and Lord Valentia who travelled in India supports this statement. He visited Poona in October 1804, and has left a very interesting record of his stay at the old Sangam Residency, his ceremonial visit to Bhaji Rao at the Shānāwāri Palace in the city in company with Colonel Close, and the great Dasera festival that month. He also visited the Peishwa at the Hira Bagh country house, of which he writes with pleasure as to its lovely situation, the view of Parbatti hill seen across the now dry lake, and the beauty of the extensive garden with noble trees, fountains, and vine pergolas. Lord Valentia, on his way back from Poona, seems to have had an interview with the young widow of Nānā Farnavis, and corroborates the tale of her beauty which General Wellesley found so remarkable. The first Sangam Residency built for Mr. Mostyn was burnt down, and Sir Charles Malet, who rebuilt it, had, while this was being done, to live in the city, camping during the hot-weather months on the banks of the Mūtha river.

It was at this Residency that Mr. Elphinstone spent the last few anxious days, knowing of Bhaji Rao's duplicity and seeing the Maharatta soldiery crowding in small camps all round our Cantonment ready at any moment to break out, while he kept the troops in hand, though continually under arms, as he was unwilling to take any overt action himself which might precipitate matters and upset calculations and intentions of Government in other parts of India (chiefly Central). Only when the situation became hopeless and Bhaji Rao's armed strength had so increased, did he withdraw, notifying the Peishwa that his conduct could only have one ending—War. It is said there was a wooden bridge over the Sangam here; this may have been built after 1809, for Salt's picture shows only a ford.

Leaving the Sangam *en route* to Ganeshkhind we pass the plain just beyond the cross roads to the city and between the main road and the Bambūrda hills, which was generally the site of the ceremonial camps when native notables visited the Maharatta court. Sir Charles Malet has left a description of Māhādaji Scindia's celebrated visit to Poona to invest the Peishwa in 1792 with a certain dignity and rank conferred by the Emperor of Delhi. Scindia's

Front View of the curious "Pānchleshwari" Temple (Hindu) at Bambūrda, Poona.

camp covered the Bambūrda plain almost to Kirkee, and was a scene of great magnificence, splendid ceremonies, and festivities, to all of which the Resident and his friends were welcomed. This plain was connected with the city and Parbatti Hill and Palace by the Lukdi bridge, a big wooden structure replaced in 1847 by the present stone bridge.

A short distance up the hillside facing us to the left, and behind the Ferguson College, are the Bambūrda rock-cut cave-temples, small, plain, but curious, of uncertain date, believed to belong to the first century B.C., and dedicated to Shiva. Behind the hostel of the Engineering College some 300 yards from the main road is to be seen a very remarkable Shivaite temple, that of Pānchleshwar, cut into a large outcrop of black rock on the plain, and so lying below the ground surface and easily overlooked. It is a large area cut down some thirteen or fourteen feet, so as to leave a great circular block standing in the centre. This again has been hollowed out, leaving a number of square pillars supporting a mushroom-like top in the centre of which stands the sacred Nandi. To the left a very deep cistern with a flight of steps down is excavated, and beyond into the rock is cut the large hall

Side View of " Pāṇchleshwari " Temple, looking down on the Mandap and showing the rock-cut cistern.

77 feet by 74 feet and 10½ feet high, containing the shrines of the five Hindu gods—Samba, Ambika, Vitoba, Rakhmai, and Ganpati—seen through a vista of thirty pillars, which were left to support the roof in carving out the living rock. The "pujaris" tell you this curious temple is 5000 years old, and it is certainly older than the Bhāja cave-temples, as it was conceived in a period when the simplest work only could be cut in the rock, requisite tools for elaborate carving and ornamentation not having been developed.

It was across the Lukdi bridge and Bambūrda plain that the Maharatta host streamed to overwhelm the small British force at Kirkee—the actual site of the conflict being about a mile and a quarter to the north of the high road to Ganeshkhind, and slightly east of the "Bullock's Hump" on the present Artillery drill ground. An old cannon stands on this open ground nearer the Government House end. It is said to mark the site of the battle, but I am inclined to think, from Blacker's history and his excellent plan of the field, that it stands near the right flank, probably where the Dāpuri Brigade chipped in. The English line stretched away from the old gun south, and from the Maharatta position, whence their guns opened, and the distance they carried in those days, it is reasonable to believe the battle started as our lines were crossing the present Kirkee race-course, and that the nullah a little south of this was the one which broke the charge of Gokla's horse.

Beyond the "Khind" or Pass, the road descends to Aundh, and was at one time the second of the Poona–Bombay highways, the first having been that via Kalās laid out by General Wellesley about the spring of 1803 and which joins the present highway three miles beyond Chinchwad, continuing along the foot of the hills under Lohgarh fort to Khandalla, a little west of the present road. The Aundh or second highway was the old native route improved by us, but not kept up long; it joins the present one a mile beyond Shelawadi station. Both have long since fallen into desuetude.

On the formation of the present Cantonment in 1819, a new Residency was built on the site of the present Post and Telegraph Offices, where the Political Agent resided till after the Mutiny, when Poona became a Commissionership, and in 1863 the Residency was destroyed by fire.

The first Government House was built by Sir Bartle Frere in the early "'sixties" at

Dāpuri where the brewery was, and there are still walks and aqueducts of those days to be seen in the grounds. The present Government House, which we know, was completed about 1871.

Our second ride will take us towards Kirkee along the present Bombay high road, passing the first European cemetery used after the country came under our rule, and where, in all likelihood, those who fell on the battlefield of Kirkee, no distance off, were buried. This cemetery stands on the river just behind Sangam Lodge, and has a memorial stone dated 1885 let into the wall to the memory of those Europeans who fell in that action. The only other inscription remaining is to a Mrs. Lodwick who died in 1819. And so on through the Royal Artillery barracks we reach the Small Arms Factory, which occupies the site where the little village of Kirkee stood. From here we get an extended view of the field of action of November 5, 1817, which practically settled the Peishwa and the Maharattas finally in this part of India. In those days the ground was more or less open from Kirkee to the "Bullock's Hump," no buildings and no cultivation broke the gently sloping stretch of ground. And here stood the little hamlet

Elphinstone told Colonel Burr to withdraw to from the old Cantonment, leaving at first 250 men to guard the Residency. It was now realized that a crisis was at hand, and we might be attacked at any moment. Bhaji Rao's forces had increased, and, believing his emissaries had sufficiently tampered with our native soldiery, he threw off the mask and launched his army against us. Our strength was then represented by the following:

Some details of Artillery: 2/1st Bombay Infantry and 2/6th Bombay Infantry (now the 112th and 113th Infantry), 1/7th Bombay Infantry, the Dāpuri Brigade (weak), two Companies of Bengal N.I. as Resident's Escort, and the old Bombay European Regiment, which had been hurried up from Bombay to reinforce Colonel Burr on Elphinstone's urgent representations. These latter arrived just in time at Kirkee. The remains of the old Peishwa's Subsidiary Force had a few years before been located in new lines at Dāpuri across the Mūla river two miles north-west of Kirkee, and was then known as the Dāpuri Brigade commanded by Captain Forde. This officer, who had been some years in Poona, had established considerable friendship and influence with Bhaji Rao and certain of his nobles, notably with Moro Dixit. These had four light guns with them, while Colonel Burr had six, and the whole total British strength did not amount to more than 2800 men. It is interesting to note that the Dāpuri Brigade sided faithfully with us, only a few going over to the Maharattas; and this brigade remains as it were with us still in the 123rd Outram's and 125th Napier's Rifles. On the morning of the 5th Elphinstone and escort vacated the Residency just in time, as Vinchorka's horsemen swept into the grounds from the city side. He crossed the Mūla ford below his house, and again by the old wooden bridge called Holkar's, and joined Burr at his camp. At this time, 4 P.M., it was plainly seen the Maharatta hosts were advancing from Bambūrda, and with offensive action in his mind Burr left one battalion, namely 2/6th, less its Grenadier companies and two guns posted at Kirkee, to guard the camp and to form a rallying point if necessary. He then moved forward in line with the other regiments, the Bombay European Regiment in the centre with the Resident's Escort, on the flanks the 1st and 7th Bombay Infantry, and two guns with each. Word was also sent to Forde to advance his Brigade towards Burr's right flank and so prevent the

Maharattas, numbers of whom were seen moving over the nearer hills, from cutting in between Burr and Forde. After advancing about a mile, or roughly about where the Royal Field Artillery Mess now stands, he wheeled a bit to his right to get more parallel with the hostile front, and was joined a little farther on by the Ḍāpuri Brigade, which, while *en route*, were charged by a body of cavalry under Moro Dixit. The Brigade rapidly forming into line repulsed the charge, and Moro fell, killed, it is said, by a cannon-shot directed by his friend Forde. The force then continued its advance just across the present racecourse and railway line when the Maharatta guns opened. Afterwards it was learned Bhaji Rao's heart failed at the eleventh hour, and Gokla who commanded was enjoined on no account to fire the first shot; also while leaving the city the breaking of the staff of the Juri Patka (Maharatta saffron-coloured standard) was regarded as of ill-omen. Gokla, however, had opened the ball and continued with rockets, while he sent strong parties of horse round both flanks of the English, generally making so rapid an advance that his infantry were left behind; all except a regular battalion under De Pinto, which, coming by a shorter route, suddenly emerged from trees and hedges in front of the 7th N.I. and began to form steadily. This was too much for the 7th, who moved forward to close, and so became detached from the line. Gokla seeing this sent a huge mass of 6000 horse headed by himself against them, and his guns ceased firing as the cavalry came thundering down across the front against the 7th. These stood firm, reserving their fire; and a swampy ravine, into which the leaders and masses of horsemen fell, Gokla's horse being killed under him, broke the charge.[1] The 7th had formerly been Colonel Burr's own corps, and he at this critical moment placed himself with them alongside of their colours. His two orderlies were shot by his side, his horse's head was grazed by a ball, and one went through his shako. His men now fired into the disorganized mass with great effect, only a few got within touch of the bayonets, while some galloped round and tried to attack the 6th at the village. These, however, were driven off with a few rounds from the guns stationed there and from a company of Europeans sent to help. The right flank of the line had meanwhile been charged by some

[1] This commander, a most capable, gallant man, had in 1803 fought for us alongside of Wellington at Assaye. He was killed in the cavalry fight at Ashta in February 1818.

3000 Arabs and Gosains, but the steady discipline and firing of the Europeans and of the 1st Bombay Infantry had repulsed them. At the failure of their great charge the Maharattas, completely disheartened, began driving off their guns; and Burr's little line again pushed forward, clearing the remaining enemy off. Next day the troops from Serur reached Kirkee. Bhaji Rao had spent the day at the Parbatti temple, where the window from which he watched the distant fight and saw his defeated troops break up, is shown to visitors. His flight with a large force southwards was the cause of a few other actions by various columns sent in pursuit. The losses in this battle were only 86 on our side and some 500 odd on that of the Maharattas. It did not last long and can hardly rank with some of the harder-fought actions of that period, but it had great political results—the Maharatta power in this part of India was over, and the country now came directly under the English Government.

The Maharattas treated such English as fell into their hands with brutality. Two cases of this occurred near Poona when officers were proceeding to join Colonel Burr's force just before the battle of Kirkee. Urulli, a few miles east of Harapsa, had been reached by two officers—Cornets Hunter and Morrison of 1st and 2nd Madras Cavalry respectively—and an escort of twelve sepoys coming up from Dharwar, unaware of Maharatta hostility. They were attacked by a body of the Peishwa's men, and seizing a choultry in the village, defended themselves in it, by using baggage for barricading till their ammunition ran out. The Maharattas gained the roof and made holes through which they shot down most of the sepoys. The rest were taken prisoners and hurried off to Fort Kanguri in the Konkan, and thence six weeks later to Wassota fort near Satāra, where our columns eventually released them, after they had endured much severe treatment and hardship.

Captain Vaughan, 15th Madras Native Infantry, and a young brother just joining the service, who were coming up from Bombay to Poona at the time, reached Wadgaon village, where they were made prisoners by a Maharatta official named Bābji Punt Gokla.

The unfortunate young men were treated most brutally, being forced forward under the lash as far as Talegaon, where Bābji Punt eventually hanged both on a tree at the Poona edge of the village. A stone put up later, but

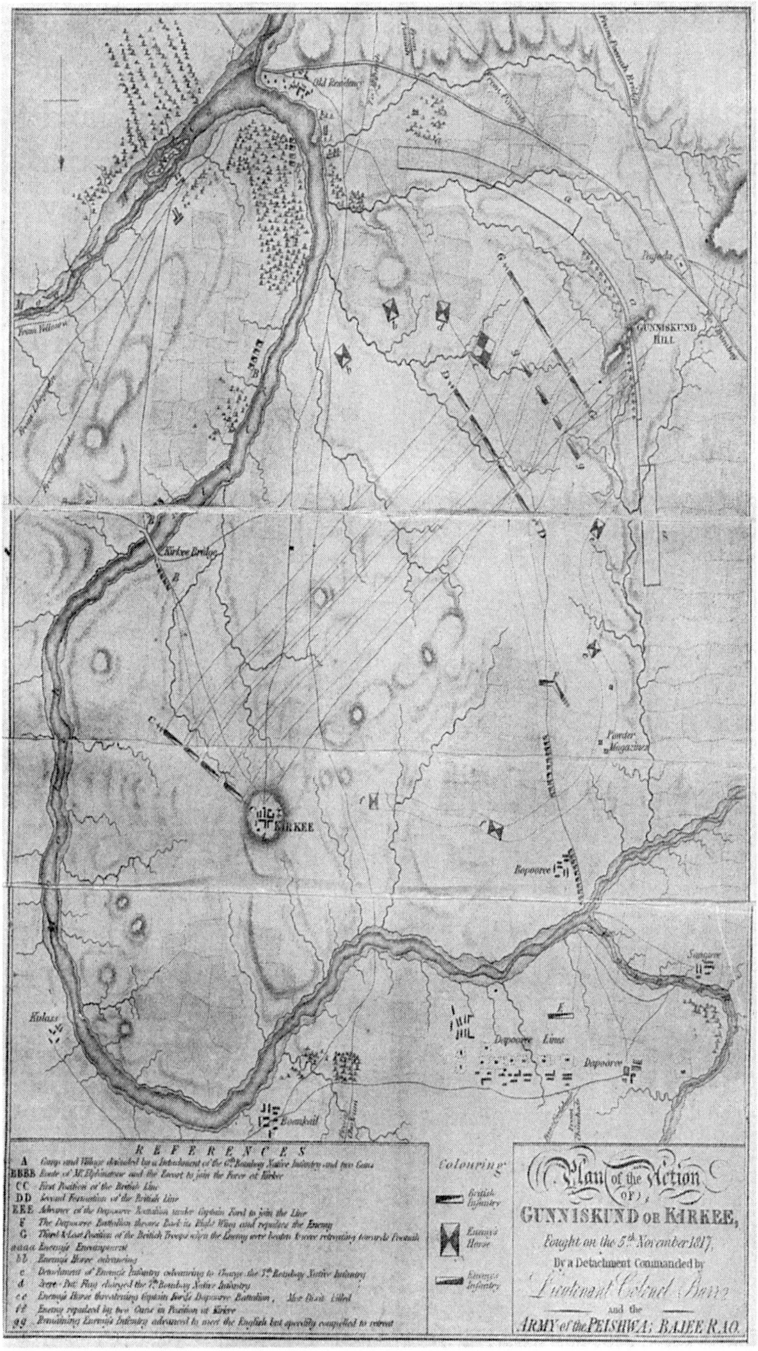

To face page 30.

now fallen into utter ruin, commemorates the incident, and Grant Duff tells us this villain was eventually caught and imprisoned for years in a wooden cage up in Singarh fort; while Colonel R. G. Burton has given an account of the death of the Vaughans in one of his pathetic tales, "Graves by the Wayside," which appeared in the *Pioneer* some years back.

Returning in our ride this day we pass what is now called the "Bund" Hill, but earlier known as "Picquet Hill," and the bridge by Yerrowda village. In those days there was a ford only, slightly below the bridge; and this was the scene seven days after the fight at Kirkee of a sharp combat, when Burr's force reinforced from Serur moved from Kirkee to attack the remainder of the Maharatta force, who were now holding a line with their left on the destroyed cantonment of "Gārpir" and their right towards Ghorpuri. Burr also wished to place himself so as to meet the march of the 4th Division from Ahmednagar and prevent the Maharattas from intercepting it. These reached Kirkee on the 13th, and next day took place Milne's combat at Yerrowda ford. The "Bund" Hill was held by the Bombay Regiment with a 6-pounder gun and efforts were made to get the force across, but the guns could not be got over as the ford had been made impassable by the Arabs in the night. Next day pioneers were set to work to repair the ford, and the day was passed in skirmishes with the Maharatta horse. On the 16th the enemy in masses came down to oppose the crossing, and after a contest of some hours Milne's left wing succeeded in crossing and establishing themselves with a few guns on the right bank. Here he had to ward off further attacks, while the bulk of the force crossed and forming line drove back the Maharattas, whose losses were very considerable, while ours were 15 killed and 68 wounded. General Smith arranged for a general attack next day, and at daybreak our cavalry moving forward, found the Maharatta lines vacated—the enemy having retreated south over the Bāpdeo Ghat to join the flying Peishwa.

Our force was then encamped, one half by the old "Gārpir" Lines, the other beyond the Sangam on the Bambūrda plain commanding the city. A successful effort was made by a Captain Turner with four guns, a party of Irregular Horse, a Light Battalion and Light Companies of the 65th Foot and Bombay European Regiment, to overtake a number of

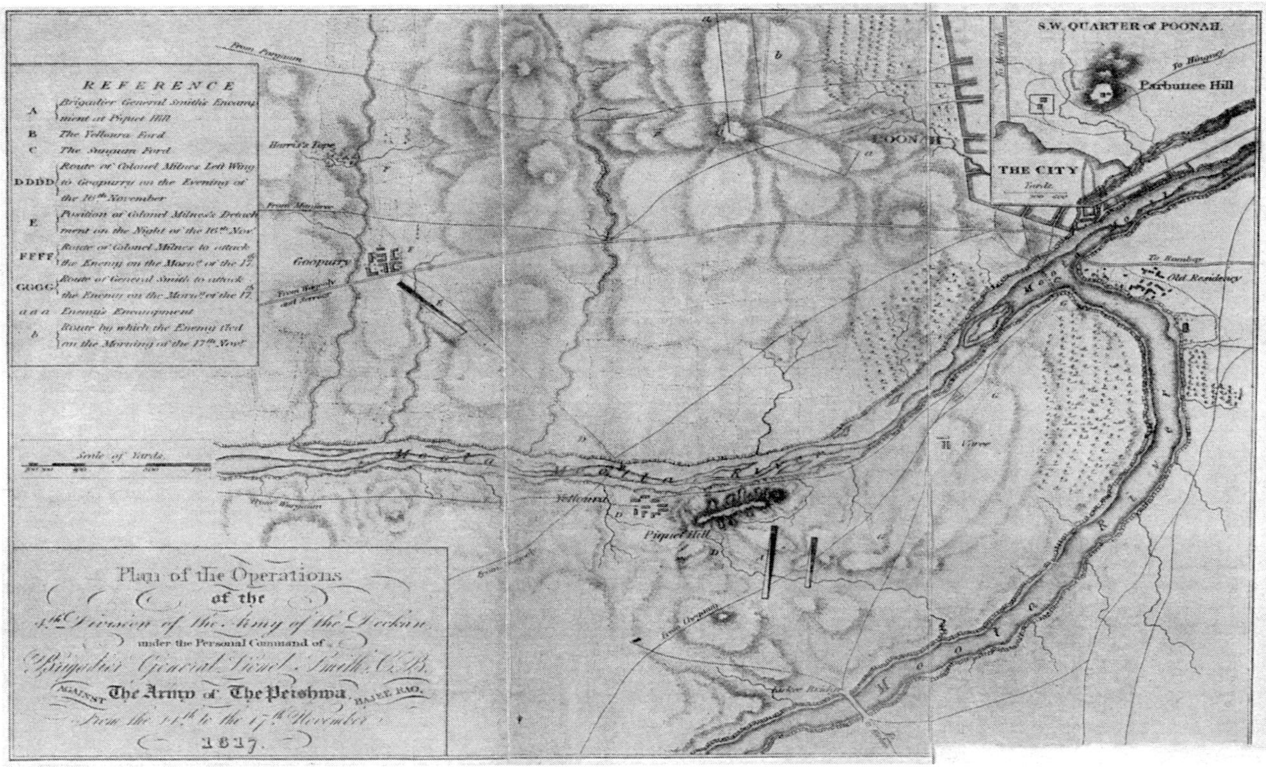
S.W. QUARTER of POONAH
Parbuttee Hill
THE CITY
POONAH
Old Residency
Piquet Hill
Yelloura
Goopurry
Harris's Tope
Scale of Yards
REFERENCE
A Brigadier General Smith's Encampment at Piquet Hill
B The Yelloura Ford
C The Sungum Ford
DDDD Route of Colonel Milnes Left Wing to Goopurry on the Evening of the 16th November
E Position of Colonel Milnes's Detachment on the Night of the 16th Nov.
FFFF Route of Colonel Milnes to attack the Enemy on the Morng of the 17th
GGGG Route of General Smith to attack the Enemy on the Morng of the 17th
a a a Enemy's Encampment
b Route by which the Enemy fled on the Morning of the 17th Novr
Plan of the Operations
of the
4th Division of the Army of the Deckan
under the Personal Command of
Brigadier General Lionel Smith C.B.
AGAINST The Army of The Peishwa, BAJEE RAO.
From the 11th to the 17th November
1817.

Maharatta guns which report said were being taken to Singarh. These were overtaken beyond Dōnja village at the foot of the hill, when a short sharp fight ensued, and fourteen pieces of ordnance, some tumbrils, and other booty were captured. A few guns not worth bringing away were disabled and the ammunition destroyed. Perhaps a memory of this bit of work may lie in the half-buried old gun lying now close to the path at the beginning of the ascent to Singarh fort.

Our third ride we will take close in and around our own Cantonment, and see how that shaped itself.

After the battle of Kirkee in 1817 and final overthrow of the Peishwa Bhaji Rao the following year saw tranquillity restored in Poona, and it was no longer necessary for the troops to live in camp as they had been doing on the Kirkee lands since the abandonment of the old Cantonment at "Gārpir," and its destruction by the Maharattas. To accommodate them it was necessary to arrange a new Cantonment, which led to the formation of the present Military Station of Poona.

To this end the present locality was decided on, it then being separated from the city by a considerable space of open lands; and the grounds of four villages, viz. Ghorpuri, Māli, Manjeri, and Wanowri, were acquired, land-owners being compensated. The original idea of locating the first troops here in 1818 was based on strategic necessities for guarding important lines of communication. Thus an English regiment and Royal Horse Artillery placed at Wanowri were to guard the communication with Sholapur on one side, and Saṭāra via the Bāpdeo Ghat on the other; while another English regiment, and later in 1822 a Native cavalry regiment, were placed at Ghorpuri to guard routes to Ahmednagar. Native units were located much where they are at present, except that an Engineer corps occupied the site now used as the Polo ground behind "Polo Vista," until the early "'seventies," their field-works area being on the far side of the present Korigaon road, where they can still be seen. In 1822–23 Cantonment boundaries were defined much as at present. During 1819 kutcha bungalows sprang up in the new Cantonment area for the use of officers, and the present Sadar bazaar was marked out for camp-followers, tradesmen, etc. In 1826 the boundaries were slightly altered so as to exclude the locality south of the present Jewish Synagogue which was then known as the Civil Lines, where dwelt the many surveyors and civil officials concerned with the surveys and administration of the new Poona district. This was done as the Governor found many objections to including the houses of these civilians within Military limits. The Garrison Church of St. Mary was begun in 1820, and remains a monument externally of unsightliness beloved of the earlier Public Works Services. It was similarly remarked on by Bishop Heber, who visited Poona in October 1824.

With the gradual settlement of the military came need for amusement, and the first Race-course sprang into existence, being laid out as shown in an old map of 1847 near the river, roughly following the line of Mangaldas Road and its continuance along Korigaon Road towards the river, when it turned to follow the side road now leading to the Boat-house. As land and building sites came more into requirement this was given up, and in the " 'fifties " a second Race-course was laid out round the ground now occupied by the lines of the Native Infantry Regiment at Wanowri. The map of 1856 shows this, and also that a Band-stand and Afghan trophies stood near the top of this rising ground, close to where the British

Infantry Barracks north of the road now stand, and by which we may gather this locality to have been probably at that time the chief social centre and general meeting-place. In those days the ground now surrounded by the Race-course is shown on all maps as the General Parade Ground. Kirkee as a Cantonment sprang into existence about 1824, the first regiment to be located there being the 4th Light Dragoons; and from an old record in the Cantonment Magistrates' Office, in 1845 we find the first official notice relative to hunting, for hounds were then kept up by a Major Weston, 14th Light Dragoons, and were kennelled close to the present Rosherville Boat-house. In the memoirs both of Elphinstone and of Malet we find that they also enjoyed hunting, though it was not till after their day that it became a regular institution. It is from Herbert Compton's pages and those of the *Oriental Sporting Magazine* 1825–35 that we get almost the best information relative to hunting in those early days, and the formation of hunt clubs. Here we learn that the Poona "Union" Hunt was looked on as the mother of all such clubs in India. It was started here shortly after the country became settled subsequent to our becoming masters in this part of the Deccan, viz. about 1819–20, and was mostly arrived at by the state of happy affluence in which officers found themselves, through ample "batta" and prize-money. Closely following the "Union" came the short-lived "Claret" hunt at Serur, a very select and expensive community which, possibly through luxurious tendencies, did not last long. The Poona "Union" was apparently started by a well-known character then, Captain Jefferys, who with one Tom Morriss later evolved a very special detachment as it were of the old parent hunt club, and of which these two, together with Messrs. Malet and White, were the sole members. They called their detachment the "Deal Table Hunt," which flourished from 1822 to 1830, and had many old hunting songs written round their doings by Morriss, who is spoken of as "Anglo-India's first poet"—his best-known song being "The next grey boar we meet." From the Spartan simplicity of this hog-hunting quartette, in which as camp furniture only an old deal table figured, arose the curious name they adopted; and they even had a seal made of which the wax copy is now in the India Office Library, presented by Mr. Herbert Compton, into whose hands it came, the gift of an old Bombay civilian who in his youth had shared in the glories of the "Union" Hunt. The device of this seal shows the top of a common camp deal table displaying the ends of the crossed legs. Round the four sides are the names of the quartette as given before, and above the table is seen a wild boar with setting of tree and hill, the whole being flanked by hog spears, the motto being "Go it." Membership of this Deal Table Hunt came to be accounted as the blue-ribbon badge of hog-hunters during the period after Waterloo.

In this matter of the early "hunts," the *Oriental Sporting Magazine* of those days (1830) has much of considerable interest; and, as showing how wealthy some of these institutions were, cites the challenge of the Nagar Hunt to the Poona "Union" for four of their best hog-hunters to be pitted against a similar quartette from Poona for a sum of Rs.10,000. It was won, if I rightly remember, by the "Union" men, and was run near Mominabad in 1830. The distances from Poona and Serur, at which they camped, were often great, involving many days' marching. In the magazine alluded to are to be found capital accounts of campings and sport, for instance in the country between Nagar and Sholapore; which, considering the frequency of these outings, helps one the better to realize the leisure in military life, and the difference between the lack of work then compared with what occurs now, in the peaceful days succeeding the long years replete with warlike enterprise of the Maharatta and Pindāri campaigns.

Shortly after this one reads of the decline in the Poona hog-hunters' glories, due to long and successful use of their spears made by the members of the various clubs round this station, and by which the boars were almost exterminated. There are accounts in this magazine by old-time hunters and sportsmen of the cheery hunt parties at the old Sangam Residency, and many equally cheery songs beloved of the sportsmen of those days, chiefly written by Tom Morriss. Some are written in fine spirit, others in a quaintly whimsical vein, of which latter a verse of "C.'s" Hunter's Song may be given as an example of how keenly those joyous fanatics could think of nought else but their beloved sport:

> Let fools with women while away
> The precious hours of youthful day,
> Let sots with drink their senses drown,
> Let bays the studious temple crown,
> Let plodding souls heap up their dross
> And nightly dream of gain or loss;

A boar to us is comelier far
Than Venus in her dove-drawn car;
The spicy bowl we only drain
That o'er it we may hunt again;
If laurel leaves some temples twine
It is with many a furrowed line;
But give us health and game in store,
The savage panther, tuskied boar,
We wish, nor hope, nor pray for more.

Scindia's Wāri near Wanowri.

Other points of old-time interest close to our Cantonment are Scindia's Wāri, the picturesque white temple we see to the left of the road near the tanneries at Wanowri, marking where the great Māhādaji Scindia died and was cremated in 1794—for thirty-five years the most influential and powerful of the Maharatta Chiefs. He owned lands here, and the ruins near by of a palace of his are still to be seen, while his descendants still pay annual visits of ceremony to the spot from Gwalior.

Here also can be seen one of the curious

Entrance to Scindia's Wāri.

" Karez " or underground water ducts, bringing water even to this day into the Rastia Peth section of Poona City. This one was built by Anand Rao Rastia, Master of Bhaji Rao's Horse, about 1784, and brings water from some large wells and springs under the hills south of Khōndwa village along the Bāpdeo Ghat Road. This Ghat lies nine miles from Poona, and in the days of the Peishwas was the main route for communication with the south, before the Dewa and Kātraj Ghat roads were made. It then fell into disuse. Our double companies yearly camp at the top of this Pass for training, and probably few know that the old water tank at the top overhung by an ancient tree was a favourite place for assemblage by Sivaji and his marauding gangs—before he became a power, but was mostly a terror in the land. Two others of these underground water ducts are also still in use, one supplying the city from the lakes at Kātraj village, seven miles along the Satāra road, and built by the seventh Peishwa Madhorao in 1750; and the other brings water from the springs near the foot of the hills between Singarh and the Kātraj Ghat tunnel. Their masonry air-shafts can be seen along the Satāra and Karakwasla roads.

This form of water conduct is peculiar to the Mohamedans, and as these were never for any length of time ruling in this part the Maharattas must have copied it from them.—probably from what they saw in the nearest Moghul province of Aurangabad.

But the Kātraj conduit and lake deserves attention from the remarkable care and thought expended over it by these early engineers, so as to ensure a pure water-supply for the city. A series of small dams were made in all the streams flowing into the main lake; from these,

Corner in Poona City.

artificial channels led off to unite again in the main stream below the two lakes, and by means of which all the first flushings of the rains, sweeping roads, hill-sides, and village vicinities, were conducted away from contaminating the lake water-supply. This then was filled with the clean water collected later behind these dams, whence sluices were opened to permit the flow into the lakes. Practically little or no impurity could get into this water-supply, which again was augmented below the Kātraj lakes by many springs, which were conducted into the main conduit underground. This particular conduit is of masonry, and is large enough for a man to walk through. The great dam of the lake is fitted with large sluice-gates at its lower level, which were opened just before the moderate rains set in so as to ensure the sweeping away of weeds and noxious vegetable matter, before the lake was filled later with clean water.

Poona City covers a large area and is entirely unlike the cities of the north in its different style of buildings with red-tiled roofs, picturesque corners, quaint temples, and house fronts and verandahs supported by heavy timbers, often carved.

The fortified palace of the Peishwas called the "Shānạwāri" is worth seeing, with its imposing bastioned gateway and heavy iron-spiked doors for resisting attacks by trained elephants. Inside, where once various Peishwas lived in state, where scenes of luxury and debauchery and often cruelty were held, are now Police Barracks, standing in a waste of jungle and ruins. It is a pity more attention is not paid to keeping this historic interior in better order. It was in here that Bhaji Rao in 1801 murdered Vittoji Holkar, brother of Jeswant Rao Holkar the victor at Harapsa, by having him tied to an elephant's foot, and

Entrance to Shānāwāri Palace in Poona City.

watched the unfortunate man being dragged shrieking through the gates to his death in the street beyond. Vittoji was cremated by the little temple close to the bridge at Kirkee, which has since borne his name. It was also in this palace that Bhaji Rao made the treaty with the English to combine against Tippoo

Sultan just prior to 1799. The large double-storied house of Nānā Farnavis, Bhaji's great Minister, can also be seen; as well as the college for Sanscrit scholars called Vishrambagh, with a very fine carved wooden frontage, built

Walls and Bastions of the Shānāwāri Palace.

by one of the old Peishwas. A part of this with the frontage was burnt years back, and was replaced by the Bombay Government with an exact copy of the carvings.

Rastia's Peth contains the mansion and surrounding property of Anand Rao Rastia, hereditary head of the Peishwari Horse. It covers a large area which in those days housed 4100 troops; the mansion standing in the centre bears traces of an ornate coloured frieze round the top of its walls, and its Durbar hall over the main entrance, now used as a survey

Entrance to Vishrambagh Palace in Poona City.

office, is worth a visit for its very handsomely carved wooden ceiling and shapely pillars.

There is no need to describe the well-known hill of Parbatti with its spires and shrines dominating the city, for there must be few who at some time or another have not climbed the 101 steps up to them and admired the perfect view over the beautifully wooded plain below almost encircled by hills, as seen from the very window whence the last Peishwa looked towards the battlefield of Kirkee, and saw the defeat of his army. From ancient times a temple to Shiva existed on this hill-top, but the present one was built by the Peishwa Bālāji in 1749 to commemorate with gratitude

Temple on Parbatti Hill.

to the gods the fact of his wife having been cured of an obstinate malady in her foot. He also a little later built the now ruined palace at the south end of the hill and its adjoining temple, the former being destroyed by lightning not long after the battle of Kirkee. The old lake (Sarasbagh), surrounded by fine old trees, and with an island and a temple in the centre, was made in 1753 by the same Peishwa, and was, until about 1900, an exceedingly picturesque place, overlooked by the sacred hill; but modern hygiene finding in it a possible source of unhealthiness, it was run dry. In the large walled enclosure immediately below the Parbatti palace, the old Peishwas used to assemble hosts of Brahmin priests from all over India, and feed them during the Dassera festival, which ends the rainy season and opens the period feasible for military operations. Bordering the dry Sarasbagh lake on its eastern side is the Hira Bagh (now the Deccan Club), a country house of the Peishwas, standing in what must once have been a most attractive garden. Its old hall is now used as a billiard and reading room. The view from here over the water of the lake, the temple island, and up to the delicate temple fanes on Parbatti hill must have been one of singular beauty in the old days.

Not far from here towards Wanowri, and across the Karakwasla canal, is the small hill "Gūltekri," at the foot of which used to be held the elephant fights in which both rulers and populace delighted.

Bhaji Rao had a favourite way of extorting

money, confessions, etc., from victims, by tying them astride a heated gun placed in the open space in front of the main entrance, while he looked on from above enjoying the show. He was a monster of cruelty and vice, as was

View of Parbatti Hill from the Hira Bagh.

his adopted son the infamous Nānā Sahib of Cawnpore.

It has been seen that at one time French influence under a M. St. Lubin was uppermost with the Peishwa, who also had a number of French officers in his forces. In Ghorpuri lines stands an old cemetery stated to contain the graves of French officers. Only one bears an inscription, viz. "To the memory of Madame Dufreneque and certain officers names unknown." It is a pity we can find nothing to inform us as to their personalities, duties, and deaths. I cannot help thinking the spelling

Tombs of French Officers on the Shankerseth Road.

of the lady's name is wrong, and that it really is the grave of Madame Dudrenec, wife of a Chevalier of France, one of those fine old free-lances of the olden days who served the Maharattas under the leadership of the famous De Boigne, was present in many actions in this part of the Deccan, raised the first trained troops for Holkar, fought against Wellesley in the Deccan, later served Scindia at Poona, and finally surrendered himself to General Lake after the battle of Delhi, 1803. Another group of tombs of French officers can be seen to the left of the road, half-way between Wanowri and Parbatti hill. But here name tablets have

Ruins of the Peishwa's Palace on Parbatti Hill.

vanished—" memor " being the only word traceable on one of them. The larger of the two Portuguese tombs to the north of Garden Reach on the Bombay high road is said to be that of Colonel De Pinto, who commanded a regiment against us at the battle of Kirkee.

We will now turn to points of interest round Poona capable of being reached by short motor or rail trips, and of these Korigaon, a village on the Bhima river, 16 miles out on the Serur road, is one full of interest. Here it was that the present Poona Horse and the old 102nd Grenadiers won undying fame on New Year's Day, 1818. Bhaji Rao with his army was in flight, and having been buffeted about by columns under General Pritzler near Satāra, who drove him almost into the arms of General Munro's force from the Belgaum side, he turned north hoping to reach Jūnnar and the strong hill forts in that part of the country. His army had camped on the right bank of the Bhima opposite Korigaon village, where, on New Year's morning, they were apprised of the approach of a small force from Serur. Captain Staunton had been ordered to bring a small flying column—500 of the 102nd, 300 horse, and 2 guns, into Poona; and knowing nothing of the proximity of the Maharatta force, he topped some low hills a short distance from Korigaon when to his amazement the plain across the river was seen swarming with troops, and Bhaji's camp was descried with the big Juri Patka waving over it. Considerations of defence, water, and supplies made Staunton race on to seize the village before being observed. This, however, was not possible;

he had been noticed, and as he reached the village, so did numbers of Maharatta foot-soldiers, while parties of horse speedily crossed and surrounded the village. However, Staunton did manage to force his way in, and to seize certain points of vantage—such as a walled choultry, and two raised positions, on

The Memorial at Korigaon.

each of which he posted a gun, and here for twelve hours he and his 800 withstood the most determined assaults by 3000 Arabs, the best and fiercest fighters under the Peishwa. At one time the gunners with one gun were all down and the piece captured, but a vigorous charge of the Grenadiers regained possession before it could be dragged away. The entire day our men were engaged in one of the fiercest

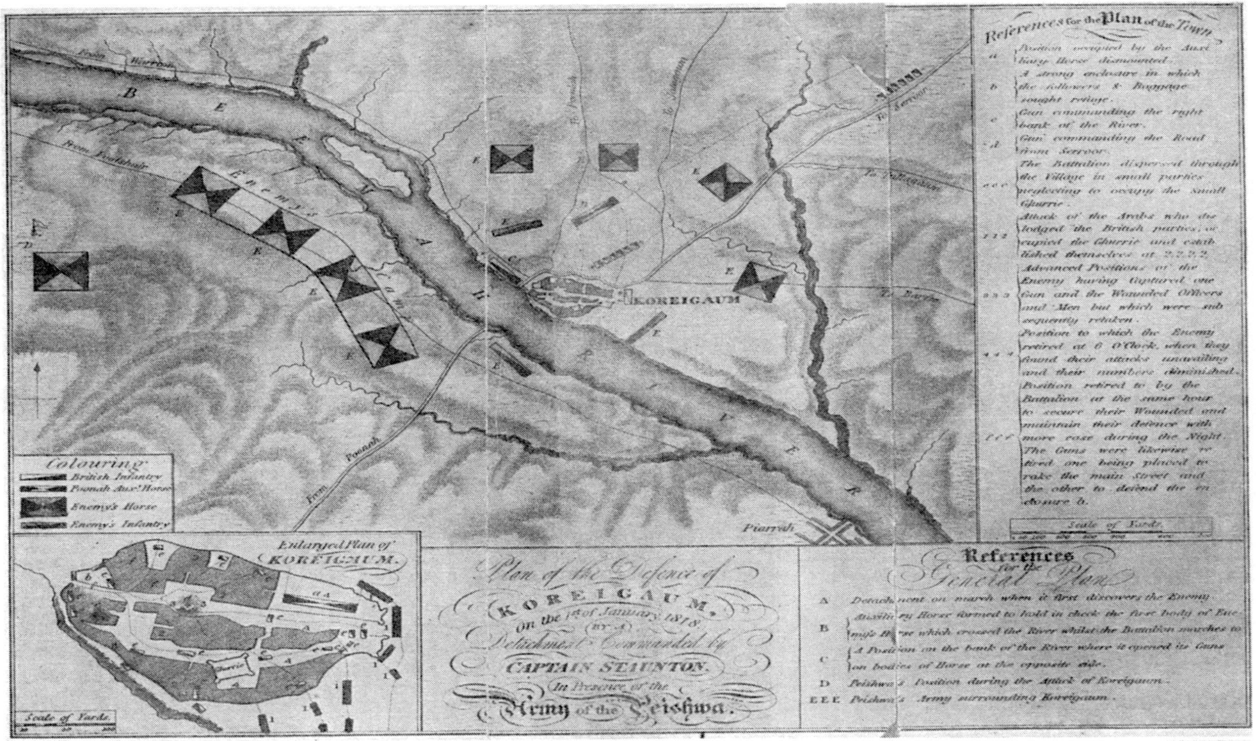

To face page 56.

of street and house-to-house fights, no rest and no water until toward 9 P.M. Bhaji Rao, hearing of the approach of General Smith's column from the north, then drew off in utter disgust at not being able to overwhelm this little force. Staunton's losses were heavy, viz. 12 killed and 8 wounded out of his 26 gunners, 50 killed and 105 wounded out of his native infantry, 96 killed and wounded out of his cavalry—total, 271 killed and wounded out of 800; and next morning, seeing his enemies draw off, and opening his two guns on them for the last time, he too retired to Serur with all his wounded. Those who visit the place can, with the aid of a map in the *History of the Maharatta War*, easily make out the points held by our men in the village. A monumental monstrosity worthy of the Public Works Department to commemorate this gallant fight was put up years ago, but, with characteristic English carelessness in these matters, it stands not where Staunton's band fought and fell, but away on the opposite side of the river, where the Maharatta force was camped.

Chākun, a prettily situated and well-to-do village beloved of the old Peishwas, lies 20 miles out on the Nasik road across the Indrayāni river. About the middle of the village stands the picturesque ruin of a fort, said by Hindus to date from the end of the thirteenth century, and originally built by an Abyssinian nobleman in the service of the Mohamedan Governor at Daulatabad, whose name is not

Ruins of Main Gate, Chākun Fort.

stated. It would appear as if this old fort was built on the site of some ancient Buddhist shrine, for Major Sanders and self going carefully over it in May 1914 found, built into the walls and the masonry revetment of the ditch, portions of carved stones similar to what are seen at the Karli caves and elsewhere. It was strengthened about 1436 by Mullik-ul-

Tijar, a Mohamedan General in the reign of Ahmed Shah Bhāmine of Daulatabad, who was sent with a force into this district to put down disturbances. The fort was nearly square, with towers at corners and centres of the high thick loopholed walls, and was surrounded by a good ditch 30 feet wide and 15 feet deep, the sides of which were revetted with blocks of masonry, and which was filled with water. The entrance was through a fine gateway, which is still partially intact on the east side, while a raised hornwork with ditch still further guarded this flank. From here Mullik-ul-Tijar controlled the turbulent district. Chākun again rose in importance when it, together with the Poona jaghir, became the charge of Malloji Bhonslay, the grandfather of the great Sivaji, in the end of the sixteenth century, and we next hear of it in 1662 when General Shaistah Khan was sent with an army by Aurungzeb's orders to punish Sivaji's aggressions. Shaistah Khan, marching from Aurangabad towards Poona, found Chākun fort blocking his way and attacked it, thinking it would capitulate at once. One of Sivaji's best lieutenants, Phirūngaji Nursalla, was in command here, and made an excellent defence against the Mohamedan host for nearly two months. The latter at last were able to spring a mine under the north-east bastion, by which a breach was made and duly assaulted. The assaults were beaten off by the gallant Phirūngaji and his men standing in the breach itself. Numbers fell on both sides, and at nightfall

Phirūngaji's Bastion, Chākun Fort.

Shaistah drew off his men. Next morning owing to his heavy losses Phirūngaji capitulated, and was treated by the Mohamedan General with the greatest respect in virtue of his gallant defence. The Maharatta leader would not listen to Shaistah's overtures that he should join them, and he and his garrison were allowed to march out and join Sivaji, by whom he was highly commended and rewarded. The Moghul troops in this action lost over 900 men, while the small Maharatta garrison was reduced to a handful, attesting the severe fighting round the now ruined walls. Five years later the place was handed back to Sivaji.

In 1685 Chākun was again the scene of heavy fighting, when Sultan Mahmoud Akbar, in revolt against Aurungzeb, was defeated by the imperial troops just outside the north end of the village.

Towards the end of Aurungzeb's reign, or about 1707, the Maharattas under Dammaji Jadow again revolted, and Lodi Khan was sent against Poona. Finding the Maharattas too strongly posted he retired on Chākun where, furiously attacked by Dammaji, he was defeated with great slaughter, the Maharattas reconquering this part of the Deccan.

Lastly we come to our own times, and find that early in 1818 Chākun fort felt the tide of war surge against it for the last time; for in the various columns sent out in the winter of 1817–18, in pursuit of the ex-Peishwa and his forces as well as in the reduction of the numerous hill forts which held out against us, we find that Colonel Deacon's column operating in the Ahmednagar district was directed to move against Chākun which had been seized by a body of the Peishwari forces. In February 1818 Deacon's column reached Serur, where it was joined by the Bombay European regiment with some howitzers and guns. The units composing the force, besides this English regiment, were the 2/17th Native Infantry, a battalion of the Nizam's force, an Engineer company, some Pioneers, and a detail of Artillery. Arrived before the fort, which was deservedly considered strong with substantial walls and defences, it was found the garrison made a show of determined resistance. On 26th February Deacon's first breaching battery was arranged for, about 250 yards off the west face, and opened; while another battery of 12-prs. was arranged for a little farther towards the south side to bring down some collateral defences. All were in action by that evening, the garrison returning the fire heartily. The following day one of the enemy's guns was dismounted, and as the breach appeared practicable, a wing each of the Bombay Europeans and 2/17th Native Infantry were ordered forward to the assault. Seeing this the heart went out of the garrison, who hung out a white cloth and gave up the place. Our losses were trifling—

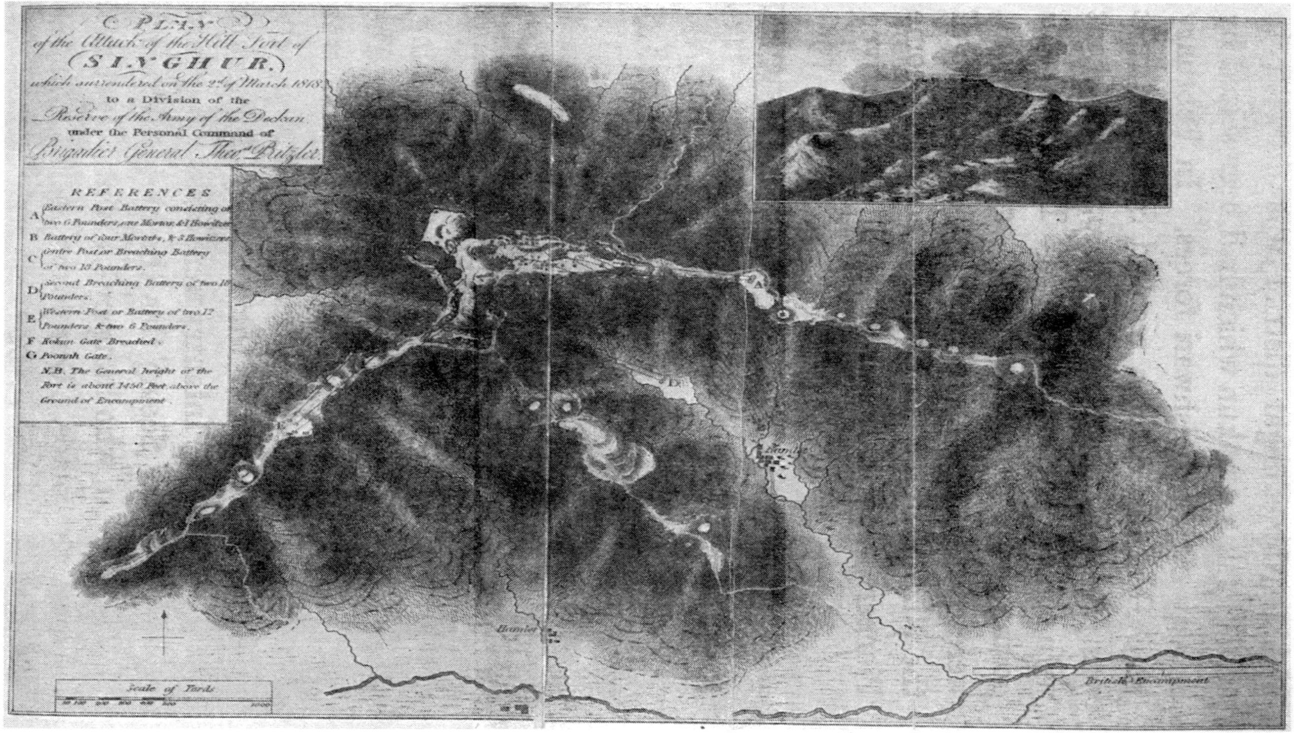

To face page 68.

six English soldiers and a few sepoys killed and wounded.

On the way out to Chākun the village of Bhosari is passed eight miles from Poona, and is worth making a halt at to see some curious and very ancient circles formed of large rough

Colonel Deacon's Breach, Chākun Fort.

boulders, and the equally curious "hero" stones set up near them, and the village. It appears that this village and locality, in the far-off past before the Christian era, was dedicated to Vetal the Ghost God, and leading members of village communities in this vicinity were brought here for burial. For instance, on one of these so-called "hero" stones is rudely carved the figure of a man lying dead with three cows above him—meaning that he lost his life in a cattle raid. On another is represented a man on foot with bow and arrows who fights three others with spears. The most

Ancient Stone Burial Circle at Bhosari.

complete of the boulder circles stands near the road on the south side, and has a grave of roughly dressed stones in the centre. The remains of several small and ancient Hindu shrines stand near these circles. Although difficult if not impossible to assign any dates to these rude enclosures, it seems certain they are monuments to the dead, bones having been discovered on digging in them, and that the ancients held this locality for some reason or other to be particularly desirable for burial purposes. Feasts were held here annually in honour of Vetal the Ghost God. Savants tell one these rude circles were the precursors of the Buddhist "stupa," or burial mound with encircling rails, and that they were originally set up to prevent evil spirits from disturbing the dead. Another of these large circles of boulders can be seen on a spur of the low hills to the east of the Satāra road and about two miles from the city.

Singarh, which we all know at least by sight, dominating the country from a height of 4600 feet to the south-west, and 15 miles from Poona by way of the Karakwasla Lake, has also heard English guns and experienced a bombardment besides that at the little fight previously alluded to at the foot of the hill. The hostilities commenced by the Peishwa in 1817 and his flight after Kirkee had given employment to a large number of our troops, of which the Reserve division was ordered south under General Munro against Satāra. This important centre of Maharatta intrigue and power unexpectedly surrendered without a blow, thus at once releasing troops to reduce the principal hill forts in this neighbourhood. Accordingly, a force of 4100 of both Madras and Bombay Artillery, Infantry, and Pioneers under General Pritzler was detailed to proceed against Singarh. They approached it from south, the main body camping in the valley below, the 2/9th Bombay Infantry and a regiment of horse being sent round to hold the north exit towards Poona. The fort is of irregular form, about 1000 yards long by 800 broad, and is of great strength, particularly on the north, where the steepness of the hill-sides precludes any possibility of successful attack. It was held by some 1500 to 2000 men. On the 20th of February 1818 the investment was started, and reconnaissance showed attacks to be feasible only on the south and west. Accordingly, working parties were distributed and batteries arranged for on the eastern and western ridges, which were gained with but slight opposition. By the 24th both batteries, containing 4 mortars, 3 howitzers, and 2 12-prs., were ready and opened their fire at daybreak. By the 27th two other batteries were arranged for on two small intermediate spurs running up to the "Konkan Darwāza," which it was intended to breach. The battery on the east ridge was located about 600 yards from the precipitous corner to the left as one climbs to the Poona gate and near the top. There are traces here of the rough road made to get the guns up by. By the 28th another battery

View of the Konkan Darwāza at Singarh, breached by the English in March 1818.

with 2 18-prs. opened fire against the southern face, so five batteries in all were pounding that side of the defences from the 24th of February to the 28th, the enemy returning the fire briskly and managing to damage seriously our battery opposite the Konkan Gate, which was repaired again by the 28th. On the 1st of March the bombardment was suspended as a white flag was hoisted, and two Maharatta officers came out to treat. Articles of capitulation were drawn up with which the officers returned, but as no reply was received after three hours the guns opened again, and on the 3rd of March, it being seen that a breach would soon be practicable, orders were issued for the assault that afternoon. A party from the fort, however, arrived about noon, and terms were finally arranged. Edward Lake, in his *Sieges of the Madras Army*, tells us that 8 18-prs., 5 mortars, and 2 howitzers expended 1417 shells and 2300 18-pound shot during this siege. The losses on both sides appear to have been trifling. It is recorded that the prize property found in this fort amounted to 50 lakhs of rupees and a valuable golden image of Ganesha—it would be interesting to know what became of the latter.

In Singarh fort stands a memorial put up by Sivaji in honour of his great friend Tannaji Malūsre, who was killed in the famous escalade of the place in 1670. The account of this daring enterprise can be found in Grant Duff's history. Briefly, the fort was held for the Moghuls by a celebrated soldier Uday Bawan, with a choice body of Rajput troops numbering some 2000 odd. Determined to seize this important stronghold Sivaji sent Tannaji with a selected 1000 of his favourite Māwuli foot-soldiers against it. These, proceeding by wooded valleys from Rajgarh, arrived below Singarh unnoticed by the enemy, and selecting the most precipitous and difficult corner, viz.

Memorial Stone to Tannaji Malūsre in Singarh Fort.

that which we see to the right facing the hill from Poona, as being less likely to be well watched, they climbed after dark to the foot of the rock. Here Maharatta accounts say that Tannaji sent up a "Gorpar," the large iguana lizard, with a light cord round it. The creature reached the top, when the cord was twitched and the frightened "Gorpar" clung firmly to the rock so that a light youth could climb up with its assistance. He then lay down, and pulled up the light cord to which stout ropes were attached and made fast to a rock. The Māwulis then quietly ascended, each lying down as he got in, and some three hundred odd

The Poona Gate at Singarh Fort.

were thus waiting with Tannaji when something attracted the attention of the Rajputs, and one advanced who was immediately brought down by a Māwuli arrow. Hoping still to surprise the garrison, Tannaji's party dashed forward to be met by a large party of Rajputs armed, and in the fierce hand-to-hand struggle Tannaji was slain, and his men were pressed back to where the ropes were. Here Sooryaji, their fallen leader's brother, had already ascended with most of the remainder, and learning of Tannaji's death he rallied the Māwulis to avenge his loss, and declared the

View along the Great Dam of the Karakwasla Lake, below Singarh.

ropes leading down had been cut away. The Maharattas dashed forward again, their war-cry "Har Har Mahadeo" resounding through the fort, and with a supreme effort overcame Uday Bawan's men. They then arranged a bonfire which was to signal success to Sivaji watching at Rajgarh through the night, and when morning broke it was found over a third of the Māwulis had been killed, and close on 600 Rajputs. Sivaji grieved long over the loss of his friend Tannaji, who was cremated where the stone now stands and where his widow committed "suttee"; and to every one of the remainder of the escaladers he gave a silver bangle in memory of the action. I have been told some of these are still to be found amongst the descendants of those formidable Māwuli soldiers, who regard them as venerated heirlooms.

Leaving a garrison of two companies of Native Infantry at Singarh, Pritzler next moved against Purandhar fort, having a sharp action at, and bombardment of, the fortified palace in Sāswad town; the marks of the shot being still seen all over the east wall, which, of extraordinary thickness, resisted the bombardment. The place, however, soon gave in, and the column turned against Purandhar, which appeared a stupendous task, powerful fortifications crowning the curiously scarped hill-tops of Wazigarh the lesser, and of Purandhar the main fort. With infinite labour guns were dragged up what we call the Sāswad spur, and two batteries pounded Wazigarh for three days, when it fell; and as this fort more or less commanded the main one the Maharattas capitulated with slight show of resistance. Sāswad and Purandhar are both well worth visiting, being only 20 and 27 miles respectively from Poona. A good motor road leads to the foot

East Wall of Sāswad Palace with English cannon-shot holes of March 1818.

of the hill, whence a climb of $1\frac{1}{2}$ miles brings one to the Bini Darwāza in the wall of the lower fort. The upper or main fort, with its bastions and gateways, is of great strength, and from the ancient Hindu temple at the highest point (about 4600 feet) a magnificent view is obtained, ranging over Kirkee to Lohgarh in the north, and to Satārā and Māhābleshwar in the south, the intervening area being filled with a tangled mass of lower hills and valleys. This old fortress has seen much severe fighting and many sieges, notably that of Dilere Khan, one

General View of Purandhar Hill and Fortress.

of Aurangzeb's best Generals, when in 1665, after weeks of cannonading from the Wazigarh hill and a furious attack by the Moghuls up the spur on which the hospital now stands, Sivaji had to capitulate. There is a story concerning the building in olden times of the upper gateway overlooking the hospital. No stable foundation seemed possible and the gateway collapsed several times. Priests then advised the wealthy Purandhari Raja that the burial of a large sum of money might ensure stability, and several lakhs of rupees were sunk

View of Wazigarah Hill looking down on Convalescent Depot from south-east bastion of Purandhar.

in the ground, but to no effect. At last, at priestly advice, the Raja caused a little boy and girl to be buried one on each side of the gate, which from then on remained strong in position. The story of the buried treasure, so strongly believed in by the people, caused Government to permit a party of Pioneers many years ago to proceed there and excavate for the supposed treasure, but the priests from the temple on the hill above begged for discontinuance of the work, their request being acceded to.

A small pamphlet has been written on this

Temples at Sāswad.

interesting old fortress by a former Commandant which will be of use to visitors, who can obtain it from the Convalescent Depot there.

The Rest House at Sāswad was formerly another country residence of the Peishwas, and here, after Napier's campaign on the lower Indus, the chief Mirs of Scinde were interned.

Perhaps it is not generally known by those riding, driving, or hunting near Harapsa, three

Temple in Sāswad Palace.

miles out on the Sholapur road, that this ground was in 1802 the scene of a remarkable battle between Jeswant Rao Holkar, and Scindia with Bhaji Rao's combined forces. The former, whose brother had been barbarously murdered by Bhaji Rao, came from Ahmednagar against Poona, but finding Scindia's force barring the direct route he made a detour via Jejuri, and rapidly descending the Rājwāri Pass (where the Belgaum line now runs) was able to reach a point near Loni unopposed. Scindia's force not meeting them near Serur, had returned to Poona and camped about Ghorpuri. On the 25th of October the two forces approached each other—Holkar having 14 trained battalions in 3 brigades under English officers, notably Colonel Vickers and Majors Armstrong and Harding, with 25,000 cavalry and 5000 regulars. Scindia had not much less officered by Frenchmen, but inferior in infantry. The fight opened at 9.30 A.M. a little south-east of Harapsa village with a fierce cannonade, and Scindia's cavalry in a grand charge discomfited the opposing force, who were with difficulty rallied by Holkar in person. These eventually got the upper hand. Meanwhile Vickers' brigade had routed six of Scindia's units who had no Europeans to lead them, and were then confronted by four veteran battalions of De Boigne with four French officers. These stood their ground, and a very stiff fight took place until three of the French officers were killed and a charge of cavalry led by Holkar broke them up with heavy loss. Complete success attended Holkar, who captured the bulk of Scindia's guns, baggage, and stores. Bhaji Rao fled to Singarh with some 7000 of his men. Holkar humanely declined to enter the city and withdrew his victorious troops after the fight; whereupon some battalions flushed with success pressed on to pillage and loot the city, and it is said were only stopped by Holkar advancing some of his guns near Wanowri and turning them on to the mutinous troops, which brought them to heel. A fresh treaty being not yet completed between the English and the Peishwa, owing to the latter failing to pay for the upkeep of the Subsidiary Force, these took no part in this affair, but were in their lines at "Gārpir" with the opposing cavalry at the end of the battle, fighting close round the Cantonment. Colonel Close had displayed the British flag at prominent points, which was respected. Immediately after this the Peishwa sent a definite agreement binding himself to cede 25 lakhs of annual revenue for the proper support of the British Subsidiary Force. Colonel Close, the day after the battle, paid a visit to the victor, and records how he found Holkar in a small tent, ankle-deep in mud, wounded in the body by a spear and with a sabre-cut in the head which he got from an artilleryman in one of the charges. It was this redoubtable Chief who opposed Lake in the battle of Delhi the following year, and who was later pursued to the Sutlej where he surrendered. Bhaji Rao fled to Bombay, where he made fresh agreements with Government called the treaty of Bassein, by which he sacrificed his independence as the price of British protection.

The Bombay–Poona road, which, in the vicinity of Chinchwad and Talegaon, we know so well from manœuvres, has also seen stirring times, when in 1778, in order to counteract French intrigues and establish English influence, the Bombay Government sent their first force into this part of the Deccan.

The Government's force sent in 1778 consisted of 591 European soldiers, 2300 sepoys, and 1500 gun lascars with various sorts of guns under command of a Colonel Egerton, and it came to signal grief through dilatoriness and mismanagement. The advance guard of six Grenadier companies of Native Corps reached and established themselves in Khandalla on the 22nd of November, 1778, under a Captain Stewart, who proved the one shining light in a tale of disaster, and whose name still figures in Maharatta village songs as "Stewart Phākray" or Hero Stewart, from the way he and his held out alone against the Maharattas, enduring numberless fights and losses during the month in which the supine Egerton sat at Panwell, unable either to make up his mind or formulate plans. Stewart was killed in a sharp fight just below the Karli Caves in the first conflict after the main body reached Khandalla on the 4th of January 1779, and when Egerton at last advanced on to the plateau. His progress like his mind was slow even to apathy, and was made at a remarkable rate of three-quarters of a mile a day, which gave the enemy constant opportunities of harrying his force and causing considerable losses. Māhādāji Scindia and the Peishwa had sent forward their main body of 50,000 troops to Chinchwad, expecting daily to meet Egerton; but as he did not appear this force again advanced to near Talegaon, 22 miles from Poona, and where, in mid-January, Egerton's force arrived. Here, confronted by Scindia's army, his heart failed him; and in spite of information brought by reliable spies that the enemy did not intend to give battle, and the entreaties of some of his officers, Egerton suddenly ordered a retreat, stating that the numbers and determined attitude of the enemy did not justify his attacking. The fatal orders were given, the retreat began, and so did Scindia's advance; for he, gauging the situation, hurried forward his horse who closed round Talegaon before Egerton could get clear. During the night the Maharatta infantry arrived, and Egerton, to facilitate his movements, had most of his guns thrown into the lake to the south of the village. At mid-day on the 12th of January Scindia's infantry had reached the vicinity of Wadgaon and engaged Egerton's advance guard as they approached that village. The English column all that day was heavily attacked on all sides, the weight of the chief assaults falling on the late Captain Stewart's companies and two guns, now commanded by Captain Hartley. This detachment again fought splendidly, the records say even drawing admiration from Scindia himself, who said, "That red wall builds itself up again as soon as bits of it fall down." Hartley's supreme efforts kept the Maharattas at bay until Wadgaon was gained by the now almost demoralized main body. Here for a day the force had a little respite till Scindia's guns got on to the place, and his infantry were able to effect an entrance. On this Egerton and Cockburn deputed Mr. Farmer, a civilian secretary, to treat. The terms Scindia imposed were humiliating, and implied the handing over of all English territory acquired since 1772, together with the revenues of Broach and Surat, and the giving up of certain Maharatta chiefs who had fought on our side. Hartley pleaded in vain for one more big "scrap," but Mr. Carnac, the civil official with the force, went to Scindia and concluded the treaty on these disgraceful terms. Certain English officers were left as hostages, and the beaten dispirited troops retired on Bombay, where Government at once repudiated Carnac's treaty of Wadgaon.[1] The English prestige and position were not long after restored by General Goddard, who, after his remarkable march across India with a Bengal Division, hammered the Maharattas at Surat, and at Bassein near Bombay. He then proceeded towards Poona, and after a successful action near Khandalla the Maharattas caved in and executed another treaty with the British Government.

Here let me digress, as the mention just now of Captain Stewart's place of decease, Karli, brings to mind the very ancient and remarkable shrines of worship here, which can be

[1] It may here be noted that the village of Wadgaon has otherwise a historical interest in the fact it is the place of origin of the famous Holkar family.

visited in a day's outing by rail to Lonavli, and thence a tonga drive of 5½ miles, or direct by motor from Poona. These rock-cut temples and "viharas" are reached after a short climb from where the tongas are left, and are eminently worth seeing. The main temple is exca-

Interior of Chaitya at Karli.

vated far into the solid rock with a degree of exactness and grace which makes one marvel how the work was ever accomplished with only the rough chisels and hammers of the pre-Christian era. Professor Kennedy, who has gone deeply into this interesting subject, states the only tools used by the ancient Hindus in these gigantic undertakings were simply a small chisel and an iron mallet, the former often made tapering to a fine round point, and the head of the latter having a deep hollow filled with lead. "With such simple tools," he says, "they scooped out the granite rock and fashioned the artificial caves into the

Entrance in hill-side to the Karli Chaitya.

marvellous works we now see. It is most improbable that the early Hindu workers in stone had any other implements." In this laborious way have they left imperishable memorials of their patient skill; and the wonder is, considering the length of time taken to complete any of these works, which probably no man ever saw begun and finished in his lifetime, that these operations were carried through to the fulfilment of the original ideas. Every portion far into the cave recesses is in keeping with the first ideas, which naturally show themselves near the outer surface of the rocky hill-sides, and the main intention must have been most carefully impressed on each succeeding superintending architect and workman.

Four miles across the valley is another set of cells, and a temple at Bhāja, three-quarters of an hour's walk from Malavli Station, which should also be seen. The latter temple is smaller than that at Karli, but the whole setting of these caves is far prettier, being on a wooded hill-slope closely overlooked by the frowning walls of the Visapur and Lohgarh forts.

A peculiarity of the Bhāja excavations lies in the group of fourteen huge dāgobas, memorial or relic monoliths cut out of the solid rock and left standing on the open hill-side. Ferguson puts the date of the excavations at Karli at about the year 80 B.C., those at Bhāja 120 years earlier, and says they may have occupied 40 to 50 years in the making. Before visiting these interesting places it would be well to look into Ferguson's and Burgess's book on Indian archaeology for a detailed description.

Seventeen miles out on the Bombay road from Poona, viz. on the north end of Shelawadi hill, and reached by a short climb to the saddle connecting the smaller with the larger hill, another series of "viharas" and a plain unadorned "chaitya" or temple can be seen.

Dāgobas cut out of the rocky hill-side at Bhāja.

These are Buddhist, though in later days votaries of Shiva have used the temple and set up an altar and a Nandi, and are of earlier date again than those previously mentioned. They are cut into the face of a precipitous rocky hill-side overlooking an extensive and beautiful view across the fertile Pauna valley to the hills of the Ghat Mahta, and can be visited in an afternoon's motor or bicycle run.

According to Ferguson and Douglas these rock-cut temples, with their marvellous carvings, in many cases as clear-cut still as if the work of a few years back instead of thousands, were preserved, after the Buddhist religion and its votaries had passed away, by falls of earth which blocked up the entrances and so preserved the stone from the wear and tear of weather. But they do not tell us who searched for and uncovered them again, which it would be interesting to know. We only came to Bombay in 1669, and yet ten years later the cave-temples at Kanheri in Salsette were known to us, as witnessed by the names of an Englishwoman and three men (John Butfer, Anna Butfer, K. Bates, John Shaw) carved on the leg of one of the huge figures of Buddha with the date 1678. Messrs. Wales and Daniel, two painters who visited India between 1790 and 1800, are the earliest English to depict these marvels of ancient times which had then been, it would seem, uncovered; and the only European before them who saw and recorded his impressions of any of these old places of worship seems to have been a Frenchman, Monsieur Thevenot, about 1666. Did he start a series of excavations, and how did he know where to begin?

Those visiting Talegaon should not fail to continue some three miles along the Nasik road, where the fine old Moghul fort of Induri stands, guarding the ford of the Indrayāni river, now spanned by a masonry bridge.

Interior of Induri Fort and Main Gate.

In the early part of 1803 General Wellesley was with a portion of the Madras Army in the neighbourhood of Bellary, where he had been settling the country after his successful pursuit of the notorious Maharatta freebooter, Doondia Waugh, when a few months earlier dissensions and trouble arose in Poona. Holkar and

Amrut Rao both had designs on the place in the absence of the Peishwa Bhaji Rao, who, after the defeat at Harapsa, had fled to the English in Bombay, and was still absent. Wellesley was therefore ordered north with a force of 9700 men, including one European cavalry and two European infantry regiments, and started from Hurryhar on the 9th of March 1803, and on the 15th of April was joined on the Nira River by Colonel Stephenson with the Nizam's Subsidiary force. The latter was then detached to head off Holkar's force coming south from Nasik, while Wellesley went on to Poona. Urgent advices from the Resident reached him to push on and save the place from being sacked and the Peishwa's family from injury. In response to this Wellesley on April 19th-20th made his famous march of 60 miles in 32 hours from Bārāmatti with 412 English and 1297 Indian troops, approaching down the lesser Bhore Ghat (the Rājwāri pass on the S.M. Railway), and appeared before Poona at the head of his cavalry on the 20th of April, when Amrut Rao (Bhaji Rao's brother) drew off declining a conflict, Holkar's aid being still afar. Wellesley then said of himself that he had outdone the Maharattas themselves in rapid marching, and when we consider the heavy cloth uniforms of those days, and the packs the men carried on them, the achievement was a notable one. Wellesley's force was encamped here for some time, and it was during his stay here that he laid out the high road running through Kalās to Shelawadi and on down the Bhore Ghat.

Induri Fort from the river.

This latter descent his working parties graded and generally made easier, though for some twenty odd years after it was still too steep for carts, and Bishop Heber mentions having in the early "'twenties" to leave his carriage at Kampoli and walk up to Khandalla at the top, coolies carrying his baggage, till he got another carriage and was able to drive on to Poona. He speaks generally in praise of the highway from Bombay to Poona, with the exception of this ascent, which was then so steep that all travellers either walked or rode up, merchandise being carried up by coolies, fresh carts or carriages being obtained at the top. It is curious for us to find him recording then that "the road with all its inconveniences is probably sufficient for the intercourse which either is, or is likely to be, between the Konkan and the Dekkan," and to compare his statement with present-day conditions and needs. About 1826 it was re-aligned and improved by Sir John Malcolm. In late May 1803 the Peishwa Bhaji Rao was escorted back to Poona from Bombay by an English force of 2400 of all arms, including a wing each of the 78th and 84th Regiments under Colonel Murray, 84th Foot, attended by Colonel Close the Resident. In the Marquis of Wellesley's *History of the Maharatta War* it is recorded this force passed General Wellesley's camp in the vicinity of Dāpuri, when a halt was made for interchange of courtesies. A week later the Peishwa was formally installed on the "musnud" with much ceremony, and amid the roaring of salutes fired by all the troops, English and Maharatta, in and around Poona.

The sight of a Maharatta camp and line of march presented a remarkable spectacle in those days. Mr. Elphinstone, before becoming Resident in Poona, was at one time on Wellesley's staff in the Intelligence Service, and was present at Assaye, Argaum, and Nagar, and vividly describes the spectacle of a Maharatta force. Their camp, he says, was an assemblage of every sort of tent of every shape and colour, spreading for miles over hill and dale. When they marched, a sea of horse and foot poured over the country, often 15 miles long by 2 or 3 broad, with waving flags, beating tom-toms, mixed with a loose struggling mass of camels, elephants, bullocks, dancing-girls, traders, etc.

While on this Poona–Bombay road the old fortress of Lohgarh, 5 miles this side of Lonavli, must not be forgotten and should be seen. It is best reached by motor 35 miles to Malavli Station, whence a fairly easy climb of some 1500 feet brings one in 4 miles to the main entrance on the south face of the hill just over the little village of Lohvadi. At the saddle between the two fortified hills of Visapur on the left and Lohgarh on the right, close to the path, is a stone "chăbutra" on which stand some roughly carved stone horses, and immediately over this, high up the cliff, is a large hole right through the rocky spur. The hill is sacred to an Arab saint, Sheikh Umar Avālia, who in far-off times, long before the Mohamedan power was established in the early part of the fifteenth century, came to these parts as a

The Upper Gateway at Lohgarh Fort.

missionary, and drove out a Hindu ascetic who dwelt here. The "chabutra" marks where the Sheikh dismounted on arrival, and the hole in the spur is said to be the mark of his spear when he defied the Hindu. He was buried on the top of Lohgarh, and his tomb is visited annually in December by thousands of pilgrims. A little beyond this point the lowest of the four gateways, storied one above the other, is reached. These gateways have powerful flanking bastions and gun platforms, and must have formed a stupendous series of obstacles for any hostile force to overcome.

The Spur at Lohgarh with Sheikh Avālia's Spear-hole.

The little plateau below the gateways, now covered with trees and jungle, was the site of the "pettah" belonging to both forts, as the many plinths found about here would go to prove. At the top, and close to the highest gateway, stands a picturesque ruined cenotaph in honour of Aurangzeb and one of his wives, and all around are plinths of dismantled buildings and caves and water-cisterns, excavated originally by Buddhist monks who were the first to make a use of this hill about the second century B.C. The hill-top is spacious and commands most superb views in every

Aurangzeb's ruined Cenotaph at Lohgarh.

direction, the most remarkable of which is seen from the north, and where one looks down on to the long rock known as the Scorpion's Tail, which with its precipitous sides juts out 1200 yards from the main hill, and had a powerful battery arranged for at the extreme end called the "Scorpion's Sting." This rock is only some 30 yards or so wide, and is protected by masonry parapets, and the guns commanded the entire country-side in this direction. A little below the highest point of the hill is to be seen a huge masonry water-tank built by Nānā Farnavis when he owned the

View looking down on the "Scorpion's Tail" Rock.

fort. Colonel Prothero's troops emptied it in their search for treasure, and as they never closed up the drain it has remained dry since. Both of these forts, which are among the most ancient in the Deccan, have seen stirring times, but most of their defences were demolished about 1848 and the guns removed. On the open ground close to Nānā's tank, which used to be the old artillery park, one can still see bits of guns and stone cannon balls hidden in the grass. Here the famous sea pirate Angria in 1713 made one of his most famous and startling feats, when, after a rapid march through the Konkan hills, he besieged and assaulted Lohgarh and captured Byroo Punt the Peishwa within. The last of this nest of pirates which had harried the west coast for years was, as stated before, stamped out by Admiral Watson and Clive with a strong force in February 1756. The fort was improved and strengthened by French engineers, and was besieged and bombarded in early 1818 by a force under Colonel Prothero consisting of strong detachments of the 2/4th and 1/6th and 1/9th Bombay Infantry, 17th Dragoons, and some details of native cavalry and infantry, with 7 mortars and 4 heavy guns. In March 1818 these arrived under Lohgarh, and a little later were reinforced by detachments of the 2/6th and 2/1st Native Infantry and 300 men of 89th Foot. A little skirmishing took place to drive in the hostile outposts, and before the guns could open the smaller fort of Vizapur gave in. Batteries were then pushed against the main fort of Lohgarh, which surrendered after a short bombardment, when several buildings were set on fire and the magazine exploded. As one climbs over these precipitous hills one cannot but be filled with wonder at the way big guns were hauled up seemingly impossible heights and got into position. Till 1846 a Commandant and a British garrison were stationed here, after which it was abandoned as a military post.

It was to this fort that Wellesley paid a visit, climbing with his staff from Lonavli to interview in 1803 the widow of Nānā Farnavis, Bhaji's famous Minister.[1] The object of the General's visit was to arrange for her pension, as a gracious act in view of the way the Minister had used his influence in favour of the English; and an old record states that she eventually drew a far larger pension from the Bombay Government, viz. Rs.1200 a month, than she was properly entitled to, owing to the General having found her exceedingly comely! In fact her name is the only one mentioned with any admiration by Wellesley of all the ladies he came across in Bombay or the Deccan, when in one of his despatches he wrote: "She is

[1] Of this remarkable official of the last of the Peishwas Elphinstone records that he was the "ablest of Indian administrators, and had he possessed military talents equal to his civil capacity, he might have founded a new dynasty." He died in March 1800.

very fair and very handsome, and well deserves to be the object of a treaty."

A little touch of human nature which we are not usually accustomed to connect with the Iron Duke.

THE END